Woman on the Front Lines

Books By Belkis Cuza Malé

POETRY

Woman on the Front Lines. *Greensboro,* 1987
Cartas a Ana Frank. *Havana,* 1963
Los alucinados. *Santiago de Cuba,* 1963
Tiempo del sol. *Havana,* 1963
El viento en la pared. *Oriente,* 1962

PROSE

El clavel y la rosa. *Madrid,* 1984

BELKIS CUZA MALÉ

Woman on the Front Lines

Translated by Pamela Carmell

1987
Greensboro
Unicorn Press, Inc.

Several of these translations have appeared in literary magazines, including *Alcatraz, Intro 14, Nimrod, The New England Review and Bread Loaf Quarterly,* and three of them—"Pandora's Box," "Oh, My Rimbaud," and "Women Don't Die on the Front Lines"—are included in the anthology, LATIN AMERICAN LITERATURE: 1960-1980, published by Farleigh Dickinson University Press, Rutherford, N.J., 1986; all are published here with the generous consent of the editors.

Typeset in 11/12 *Baskerville* by Anita Richardson; printed by McNaughton and Gunn on Glatfelter, an acid-free sheet; cloth edition handbound by Leigh Carter at Unicorn Press. Assisting Mr. Balaban and Miss Savory in the design and editing of this book were Alan Brilliant and Sarah Lindsay.

Library of Congress Cataloguing-in-Progress Data:

Cuza Malé, Belkis.
Woman on the front lines

Translation of: Juego de damas.
Bibliography: p
I. Carmell, Pamela. II. Title.
PQ7390.C8J813 1987 861 86-24956

ISBN 0-87775-202-8, *cloth*
ISBN 0-87775-203-6, *paper*

Funding for this publication was received from the Witter Bynner Foundation for Poetry, the North Carolina Arts Council and the National Endowment for the Arts.

UNICORN PRESS, INC.
P.O. Box 3307
Greensboro, NC 27402

A Series of Translations of

Poetries

SPONSORED BY

THE WITTER BYNNER FOUNDATION FOR POETRY, INC.

and

UNICORN FOUNDATION
FOR THE ADVANCEMENT OF MODERN POETRY

John Balaban & Teo Savory, *Editors of the Series*

VOLUME I

Poets of Bulgaria

Edited by William Meredith

VOLUME II

Woman on the Front Lines by Belkis Cuza Malé

Translated by Pamela Carmell

CONTENTS

EL PATIO DE MI CASA/THE PATIO AT MY HOUSE

INTRODUCTION

"The woman who went out that door (in Havana) carried a bundle of papers under her arm. When the X-ray machine examined my luggage, I feared for no object of material value. I trembled inside for my poems, clumsily camouflaged."[1] Thus began, in 1979, the life of exile for Belkis Cuza Malé. First an avid supporter of revolution in Cuba, then a censored critic of Castro's new order, Cuza Malé experienced the disillusionment and repression many came to in the years following Fidel Castro's rise to power. The poems she bundled out of Cuba report the metamorphosis of an individual faced with increased restrictions and exile and bring news of that country's change, news which outsiders might never have gotten through the press.

Born in Guantánamo in 1942, Cuza Malé was the daughter of a cement-factory worker and the granddaughter of a Catalonian immigrant whose wife, weakened by malnutrition, had died in an earlier period of political turmoil in Cuba, the general strikes of 1933. Both men encouraged Belkis to study and excel, sending her to private Catholic schools where she received a general liberal arts education and associated with children of professionals and bureaucrats.

Writing had occupied her time since she was nine when she picked out a romance novel on an old typewriter her father had managed to give her for Christmas. Her first collection of poems, *El viento en la pared,* was published in 1962. The next two collections, *Tiempo del sol* and *Cartas a Ana Frank,* published in 1963 by Las Ediciones El Puente, won honorable mentions from the Casa de las Américas literary group and publisher. Cuza Malé describes herself as a wide-eyed country girl going to Havana to receive her awards and to meet with other recipients of awards, writers from all over Latin America. At that gathering, Belkis met her future husband, Heberto Padilla, also an award-winning Cuban poet.

During this time Belkis studied Cuban and Hispanic American literature at the Universidad del Oriente, graduated in 1964 with a *licenciatura* (master's degree), and moved to Havana. She contributed articles as a critic of literature and television to a variety of newspapers and journals, including *Granma*, formerly a society rag that had been recast into a political journal after the revolution. Belkis and Heberto were married in 1966.

The indulgent mood of Castro's Cuba was beginning to disappear, however. In 1965 the literary group, El Puente, of which Cuza Malé was a part, was attacked for publishing what the censors deemed bourgeois literature, but which the group had considered within the realm of revolutionary writing. The group's leaders, José Mario and Lourdes Casals, were arrested; they and several other members were sent to camps for "rehabilitation." Then, with the death of Che Guevarra, experimental and lyrical poetry lost its champion. Castro held a hard-line, Marxist view of literature: it should educate the masses, celebrate good morals, and work for the good of the whole. It should not, he believed, be the medium of self-indulgence. Padilla's book of political commentary poetry, *Fuera del juego*, awarded the Unión Nacional de Escritores Cubanos prize in 1968, blew the lid off a tense situation. The book was published, then immediately censored and destroyed. Padilla's and Cuza Malé's lives came under great scrutiny, as did that of any other writer or intellectual who criticized the new order of Cuba.

Jailed in 1971 for his continued criticism of the government, Padilla became the focus of international outcry. Members of the Mexican chapter of PEN, such as Octavio Paz, Carlos Fuentes, and Juan Rulfo, were the first to protest. Letters from Sartre, Calvino, Cortázar, Goytisolo, Vargas Llosa, and many other writers from all over the world followed. Padilla was released after a month of imprisonment but was forced to read a public apology and condemnation of other writers, including his wife, for their criticism of the government.

Belkis shared the restraints on Heberto's life between 1968 and 1979. The two were allowed to continue their work as journalists but they were closely watched and their home was bugged. A collection of her newer poems, *Juego de damas,* was also destroyed for its political comment shortly after its publication in 1970. Although sixteen of those poems were included in an anthology *Ocho Poetas,* published in Cuba, Belkis Cuza Malé was never allowed to publish her work in her native Cuba again.

Exile has been a literary theme since at least as long ago as the laments of Ovid and Dante. Current interest in the topic is keener perhaps because it represents another way to get inside the political or social repression that governments may keep from us, or to which conventional forms of media may limit our access. In the poetry of Belkis Cuza Malé, a report on the conditions of exile and the effects of that situation on the individual combines with moments of very musical and lyrical poetry.

In working with her poetry, I have considered the special role of the translator of exile literature. In addition to the usual concerns with nuance and cultural subtlety, I have had to be alert to the tension and anxiety over loss of and isolation from the most basic form of self-identity, one's homeland, elements which draw a reader's attention and curiosity yet which are hard for a translator to render authoritatively to an audience which, for the most part, has never felt that loss.

Cuza Malé's poems come in a sort of code, in fables, and allegories, forms she chose in an attempt to elude censors. The images are cryptic, those half-formed ones of dreams or of something seen out of the corner of one's eye. That this code is sometimes difficult to break can lead to frustration for the reader; the communication between poet and reader makes more of an impact once the reader grasps the message. The translator and the reader must attempt all Cuza Malé's poems, not only the easier, lyrical ones, or face being, in the selection process, the ultimate censor, silencing her protests anew.

The poems included in this collection are selections from Cuza Malé's latest manuscripts, *Juego de damas* and *El patio de mi casa,* written between 1981 and 1982 with a grant, Becas Cintas. I've maintained the order Cuza Malé arranged her poems in, with no attempt to group them thematically.

Julio Cortázar has said of exile, "I believe that we writers in exile have the means to transcend the uprooting and separation imposed upon us by the dictatorships, to return in our own unique way the blows we suffer collectively each time another writer is exiled."[2] He suggests that "it is the duty of Latin American writers in exile to quicken, to breathe life into this information, to give it the unique corporality engendered by the synthesizing, symbolic powers of fiction: by the novel, the poem or the short story that incarnates what can never be brought to life in a telex dispatch or in the column of a news analyst."[3] Belkis Cuza Malé has used this power to bring the news about her changing homeland. While she says, "Here in the United States, in the midst of what I'd dreamed of, life vibrates differently: a poem doesn't upset anyone,"[4] her own poems belie her apparent lack of optimism regarding the power of literature, and they demonstrate the capacity of literature to bring change.

ENDNOTES

[1]Belkis Cuza Malé, "A Woman and Her Poems," in *Contemporary Women Authors of Latin America,* ed. Doris Meyer and Margarite Fernandez Olmos (Brooklyn: Brooklyn College Press, 1983), p. 93.

[2]Julio Cortázar, "The Fellowship of Exile," trans. John Incledon, *Review Magazine,* 30, September/December, 1981, p. 14.

[3]Cortázar, p. 16.

[4]Malé, p. 93.

GAME PIECES
JUEGO DE DAMAS

LOS FOTOGENICOS

Por las esquinas amarillentas de la hoja de papel,
se les ve caminar, desaparecer al doblar la página.
Habitan una isla en el trópico de la guerra,
una isla donde todos los vasos están rotos,
una isla a caballo.
Entran en los suburbios de la tarde
y en los hoteles de paso,
navegan en una cama de velas blancas,
mientras él canta y ella es un ruido más,
una ola debajo de la cama.
Mejor callarse y dejarlos que duerman
        y dejarlos que vivan
        y dejarlos que mueran.
Al pie de la foto unas cuantas líneas
atestiguan el hecho:
ninguno está seguro del otro,
pero navegan,
navegan con la isla por todos los mares del mundo.

THE BEAUTIFUL PEOPLE

Across the yellowed corners of the sheet of paper,
you can see them walking along, disappearing as the page turns.
They inhabit an island in the tropic of war,
an island where every glass is broken,
an island on horseback.
They go to afternoon suburbs
and one-night motels,
they sail a bed of white sails,
while he sings and she is one more noise,
a wave under their bed.
Just be quiet and let them sleep,
      let them live,
      let them die.
At the foot of the photo a few lines
testify to the facts:
neither is sure of the other,
but they sail,
sail along with the island across all the seas of the world.

POR EL MOMENTO

Por el momento ya no nos quedan noches estrelladas,
ni enamoraditos debajo de la luna.
Es que el duro verano lo ha destrozado todo
y ha marchitado el cesped
hasta apagar la última señal.
Un pequeño farol ilumina la escena.
Bien sé que ha sido duro y largo este verano.

FOR THE MOMENT

For the moment, we've run out of starry nights,
and love birds in moonlight.
The hard summer did it all in,
dried up the lawn
and wiped out every trace.
A small street lamp lights up the scene.
I know well enough this summer was hard and long.

LAS CENICIENTAS

Somos las cenicientas.
El señor Boticelli pintó para nosotras
las tres hadas madrinas.
No somos inocentes.
El Príncipe nunca nos ha besado.
No hemos pisado su recámara,
ni lamido su vientre.
Vivimos en la cocina,
nuestra luna es el fuego.
Nuestros pies son enormes;
un largo baño no nos vendría mal.
Andamos con sayas rotas,
con las greñas al aire
y comemos pan duro.
No somos inocentes.
Por negritas, por feas y por putas
fuimos chifladas en el certamen de Miss Universe.
Pero gritamos (las deslenguadas)
¡merde! al culo del rey
y ¡imerde! a sus ministros,
aunque ellos rabien con nuestra peste.

CINDERELLAS

We are Cinderellas.
Botticelli painted
three fairy godmothers for us.
We know the score.
The Prince has never kissed us.
We've never set foot in his boudoir
or kissed his ass.
We live in the kitchen;
our moon's the fire.
Our feet are huge;
a good long bath would do us good.
We go around with our hems torn,
hair coming down.
We eat stale bread.
We know the score.
They called us niggers, nags and whores
at the Miss Universe pageant.
But we (foulmouthed) shout
merde! to that ass of a king
and *merde!* to his ministers
though they go wild with our smell.

LA FUENTE DE PLATA

Esta tarde he traído conmigo una fuente de plata.
No sé para qué ha de servirme
pues nunca he tenido fuente de plata.
Vivimos sin estos lujos y tú me preguntas:
"¿Se venden aún esas cosas?"

Nadie te exige ahora que tengas una fuente de plata.
Ni siquiera de segunda mano.
¿Quién podría exigirte semejante lujo en estos tiempos?
Será suficiente con los buenos modales a la mesa
y la pulcritud de las uñas.
Pasadas están de moda, por ejemplo, las gracias al Señor.

Será mejor que vivas sin esos lujos
y no quieras nunca servir la ensalada del pobre
en una fuente de plata.

THE SILVER PLATTER

This afternoon I've brought with me a silver platter.
I don't know what I'll do with it;
I've never had one before.
We live without these luxuries and you ask me:
"Do they still sell those things?"

No one pressures you to have silver platters.
Not even second hand.
Who could, these days?
It's enough to have good table manners
and nice nails.
Some things, like saying grace, are out of style.

It's better to live without those luxuries,
not to want a poor man's salad
on a silver platter.

CAJA DE PANDORA

La calle es el peligro, pero avanzas sin rumbo
y te sorprendes junto a la mano de bronce
de las altas puertas. Y cuando estás a punto de ser escuchado
de cometer una torpeza,
una ráfaga de aire te detiene un instante,
te hace volver el rostro y descubres a la vieja
parada junto a ti
con su pesada jaba de yarey, donde brilla, escondida,
su caja de Pandora.
Desconfías de la imaginación, no cedes
y dejas pasar
        los argumentos del tiempo
y la sola idea del amor.

Ella continúa su paso.
Fue sólo la tentación de ofrecértelo todo.
¿Por qué no te picó el milagro de la curiosidad?

PANDORA'S BOX

The danger is in the street, but you wander on aimlessly
and catch yourself near the bronze hand
on the doors. Just as you are about to make some noise,
doing something stupid,
a gust of wind holds you for a moment,
makes you turn your head, and you notice the old woman
standing next to you
with her bulging straw bag and, shining inside, hidden,
her Pandora's box.
You don't trust your imagination and don't give in.
You let the arguments of time
and the mere thought of love
pass by.

She walks on.
She was tempted to let you have it all.
Why weren't you stung by the wonder of curiosity?

BIOGRAFIA DEL POETA

Para la biografía del poeta,
olviden el verdadero tono con que hablaba,
sus amores de guerra,
los rasgos físicos
(ojos café, nariz sin suerte),
la vida en familia,
su fórmula para conseguir enemigos,
su asombro, su pereza, su virtud.
Olviden quién lo trajo al mundo,
en qué mes y en qué año se produjo la cosa.
Tengan en cuenta solamente
las ciudades en que no amó,
el tipo de mujer que despreciaba
y la influencia de William Blake en su persona.

POET'S BIOGRAPHY

For the poet's biography,
forget the tone of voice he spoke in,
his war-time loves,
facial features,
(brown eyes, hapless nose),
family life,
the way he made enemies,
his amazement, laziness, talents.
Forget who brought him into the world,
what month and what year it happened.
You only have to deal with
the cities where he didn't make love,
the kind of woman he despised,
the ways he was influenced by Blake.

OH, MI RIMBAUD

He aquí que Rimbaud y yo nos hacemos al mar
en un gran elefante blanco,
nos perdemos en la bruma inconsolable de unos ojos
y como colegiales reincidimos de pronto
en el amor.
El me toma la mano y la rechazo con un grito.
Luego,
se abandona a las aguas
y atraviesa otros mares y otros ojos
y se queda sin mí,
me regala la cabellera roja de sus sueños,
el pálido color de sus mejillas,
un espejo.

Cuando aminore la tormenta y su caballo
descubra el camino,
volverá dueño y señor del vellocino de oro,
jovial y para entonces harto ya de mí.

OH, MY RIMBAUD

See how Rimbaud and I head for the sea
on a great white elephant,
drown in the brooding mist in our eyes
and fall like school kids
in love again.
He takes my hand; I gasp and pull away.
Then
he rides out on the tide,
sails other seas, other eyes,
goes on without me,
leaves me the red hair of his dreams,
the pallor of his cheeks,
a mirror.

When the storm has passed and his horse
finds the way,
he'll come back lord of the golden fleece,
jovial, and he'll have had his fill of me.

ASI ESTAN LOS POETAS EN SUS TRISTES RETRATOS

Así están los poetas en sus tristes retratos.
Una pluma en la mano -pavorreal o tinta seca de China.
Todavía hay un brillo lógico en sus pupilas,
o la mano suave sujeta la cabeza que no cortó el verdugo.
Creyentes o no, estoicos o rebeldes
anuncian siempre el porvenir, están en lo más alto de las rocas,
y oyen crujir el mar pero no atajan su furia,
beben el ron de las tabernas
y el amor en los labios turbulentos.
Pero lo más terrible es lo que escriben,
aquello que nadie se atreve a poner en su lengua.

Así están los poetas en sus tristes retratos.
Meditabundos o simplemente coléricos.
Señoritos de aldeas,
padres de familia,
viejos quisquillosos,
mujeres entre tiernas y mañosas.
Algunos engordan con la mala vida y el poco comer,
pero son diestros y sobreviven a sus jueces.
Algunos desechan la barba y el bigote
por la sonrisa cínica.
A espaldas de ellos se conjetura
sobre este mundo y los poetas.
A nombre de ellos se oficializa la ternura.

Así están los poetas en sus tristes retratos.
Una ventana o un parque es todo cuanto les pertenece.
Al fondo se corren las cortinas
mientras en el lecho de muerte vigila la lechuza.
Robert Browning -por ejemplo-
tenía los ojos tan bellos.
¿Y quién se acuerda del rostro de Hopkins?

AND HERE ARE THE POETS IN THEIR SAD PORTRAITS

And here are the poets in their sad portraits,
quill in hand—peacock blue or dried India ink.
There's still a logical gleam in their eyes;
a delicate hand props up the head the executioner severed.
In the fashion of the time, they compress their fervor
into the thin thread of their mouths.
Believers or nonbelievers, stoics or rebels,
they always proclaim the future,
always stand on the highest rock,
hear the ocean creaking but never head off its fury,
sip rum in taverns
and love from turbulent lips.
But most terrifying is what they write,
words no one dares put into his own mouth.

And here are the poets in their sad portraits.
Meditative or merely choleric.
Fuzzy faced kids from small towns,
family men,
fussy old codgers,
women both tender and troublesome.
Some are grown fat on bad living and bad food,
but they are clever and they outlive their judges.
Some have given up the beard and mustache,
for a cynical smile.
Behind their backs, we speculate
about this world and these poets.
Tenderness is made official in their name.

And here are the poets in their sad portraits.
A window or sunny park is all they own.
In the background, curtains are drawn;
over their death beds, a screech owl watches.
Robert Browning (for example)
had beautiful eyes.
And who remembers the face of Hopkins?

De Rimbaud hablan elegantemente los jovencitos.
Dante es el signo del terror
y Byron amó a su espejo.

Así están los poetas en sus tristes retratos.
Ahora sus rostros cuelgan de una galería
o ilustran una revista.
¿No les dice nada ese silencio?

The young speak elegantly about Rimbaud.
Dante symbolizes terror.
And Byron loved his mirror.

And here are the poets in their sad portraits.
Now their faces hang in galleries,
illustrate magazines.
Doesn't that silence tell you anything?

VOCACION DE TERESA DE CEPEDA

Ausente de este mundo,
contemplando las nevadas colinas
tras la cuales imaginaba a Dios
(porque detrás no se veía más que cielo)
ella deseó como nunca la vida
y el asombro de no saberse ciega o sorda.
El le había pedido con un grito amoroso
que volviera,
que descubriera en su rostro el viento,
que descubriera en sus manos la caricia.
Pero el corazón no triunfa,
Dios está en todas partes,
es su dueño,
su empresario,
su marido,
su hijo,
su amante,
su amuleto.
El corazón no triunfa.

Todas las mujeres son de Dios
pero él no es de ninguna.
Tarde a tarde, ella ve alzarse las colinas,
pirámides en que la nieve hace su nido,
y piensa en nosotras,
pobres muchachas de provincia,
con vocación para el hogar,
a ratos visitadas por el Diablo
y abandonadas entre las hojas secas
que caen de las sombras de los árboles.

THE PIETY OF TERESA DE CEPEDA

Absent from this world,
gazing at snow-topped hills,
(beyond them she'd always pictured God,
because all she saw was sky),
she wanted life more than ever
and the joy of not feeling blind and deaf.
He'd begged her with a loving cry
to try again,
to see the wind in His face,
to feel the caress of His hands.
But the heart does not triumph,
God is everywhere,
her master,
her advocate,
her husband,
her son,
her lover,
her amulet.
The heart does not triumph.

All women belong to God,
but He belongs to none of them.
Day after day, she sees the towering hills,
pyramids where the snow makes its nest,
and thinks about the rest of us,
poor country girls,
whose work is in the home,
who're visited from time to time by the Devil,
and left among dry leaves
falling from the shadows of the trees.

YO VIRGINIA WOOLF DESBOCADA EN LE MUERTE

La soledad y el silencio nos expulsan
del mundo habitable,
¿qué ojos mirarán sin recelos
las aguas del río en que me pudro?
¿qué mendigo robará mi único cuerpo
y para qué querrá disfrazarse de mujer?
¿durante cuántas noches seré el espíritu del pobre diablo
que acampa en Londres, bajo la llovizna?

Reconstruyo el pecado.
Me lo sé de memoria.
Un diá y otro día
apagan la lámpara central,
cierran ruidosamente puertas y ventanas
y ya nadie ofrece recompensa por nuestra captura.

Un día y otro día
el mundo se hace tan habitable
que ya no estamos en él.

Envejezco.
Bajo la máscara de gran dama subyugada
me estoy poniendo vieja,
no encuentro bella tu nariz,
tu curiosidad insaciable de silencio.
Pronto se irá el invierno para no volver
o no estaré yo aquí para esperarlo.
Seré tan vieja que se reirán de mí,
que no entenderé nada,
que esperarán con ilusión mi muerte,
para cuando todo haya sido
cubrir los espejos,

I, VIRGINIA WOOLF,
RUSHING HEADLONG TOWARD DEATH

Loneliness and silence drive us
from this comfortable world.
What eyes will look without fear into the waters
of the river where I rot?
What beggar will rob my body?
Why does he want to dress up as a woman?
How many nights will I be the spirit
of that poor devil
who sleeps on the ground out in the London drizzle?

I'll reconstruct the crime.
I know it by heart.
Day after day,
they turn out that bright lamp,
shut doors and windows with a bang,
but no one offers a reward for our capture.

Day after day,
the world grows so hospitable
that we are no longer at home in it.

I am growing old.
Behind the subdued mask of a grande dame,
I start to look like an old woman,
I am no longer charmed by your nose,
by your insatiable curiosity about silence.
Winter will leave soon never to return
or anyway I won't be waiting for it.

I will be so old everyone will laugh at me,
I won't understand anything,
those dreamers will wait on my death
so that when it's over
they can cover the mirrors,

arrastrar mi cuerpo por las escaleras,
maquillar mi nuevo rostro
y vestirme con el traje de novia
que han lavado secretamente desde antes.

No les daré gusto.
No voy a envejecer.
No voy a morir.

drag my body down the stairs,
put strange make-up on my face,
and dress me in my wedding gown
they secretly washed a long time ago.

I won't give them that pleasure.
I will not grow old.
I will not die.

METAMORFOSIS GRIEGA

Safo no fue una mujer, ni un hombre.

En medio de la flora y la fauna de una ciudad griega
y ocupados los hombres en los hombres,
Safo dibujó mar salado, *una nave*
y un barril de agua dulce.
Se hizo acompañar de su criada
y de puerto en puerto reclutó esclavos,
muchachos casi negros,
deseosos de hacer sentir el sexo.
Con alguno de ellos hizo una preciosa niña
que le ocupó el resto de sus días.

Nadie sabe cómo murió, porque ya vieja
cerró su casa a los curiosos.
La Historia asegura que envolvió su restro
en un manto de seda y que luego de pronunciar
dos o tres frases inconexas,
se transformó en una mariposa,
que aún vive, que aún aletea
junto a la lámpara,
o sobre el sombrero de Proust.

GREEK METAMORPHOSIS

Sappho was neither woman nor man.

In the midst of a Greek city's fauna and flora,
        men busy with men,
Sappho sketched a *salty sea,* a ship,
a barrel of fresh water.
She made herself go from port to port
with her servant girl to round up slaves,
dark-skinned boys
eager to make their sex felt.
Of one she made a darling little girl
who kept her busy the rest of her life.

No one knows how she died; getting along in years,
she closed her home to the curious.
History tells us she wrapped her face
in a silk shawl, pronounced
a couple of jumbled sentences,
and changed to a butterfly
        that still lives, still flutters
around the lamp
or above Proust's hat.

ESTAN HACIENDO UNA MUCHACHA PARA LA EPOCA

Están haciendo una muchacha para la época,
con mucha cal y unas pocas herramientas,
alambres, cabelleras postizas,
senos de algodón y armazón de madera.
El rostro tendrá la inocencia de Ofelia
y las manos, el rito de una Helena de Troya.
Hablará tres idiomas
y será diestra en el arco, en el tiro y la flecha.
Están haciendo una muchacha par la época,
entendida en política
y casi en filosofía,
alguien que no tartamudee,
ni tenga necesidad de espejuelos,
que llene los requisitos de una aeromoza,
lea a diario la prensa
y, por supuesto, libere su sexo
sin dar un mal paso con un hombre.

En fin, si no hay nuevas disposiciones,
así saldrá del horno
esta muchacha hecha para la época.

THEY'RE MAKING A GIRL FOR OUR TIMES

They're making a girl for our times
with a lot of lime and a few tools,
wires, artificial hair,
cotton breasts and a wood frame.
Her face will have the innocence of Ophelia
and her hands, the charms of Helen.
She'll know three languages
and she'll be very good with a bow and arrow.
They're making a girl for our times,
one who knows politics,
and a little bit of philosophy,
who doesn't stutter,
and doesn't need glasses,
who looks like an airline stewardess,
and reads the paper every day,
who has no hang-ups of course about sex
and doesn't get men into trouble.

If there are no new specifications,
that's how she'll come from the oven
this girl made for our times.

LAS MUJERES NO MUEREN EN LAS LINEAS DE FUEGO

Las mujeres no mueren en las líneas de fuego,
no ruedan sus cabezas como pelotas de golf,
no duermen bajo un bosque de pólvora,
no hacen ruinas el cielo,
no hay nieve que enfríe sus corazones.
Las mujeres no mueren en las líneas de fuego,
no expulsan al diablo de Jerusalem,
no vuelan acueductos, ni vías férreas,
no dominan el arte de la guerra,
ni el arte de la paz.
No llegan a generales,
ni a soldados desconocidos de piedra
en el centro de una plaza mayor.
Las mujeres no mueren en las líneas de fuego.
Son estatuas de sal en el Museo del Louvre,
madres como Fedra,
amantes de Enrique VIII,
Mataharis,
Evas de Perón,
reinas asesoradas por un Primer Ministro,
niñeras, cocineras, lavanderas
o poetisas románticas.
Las mujeres no hacen la Historia,
pero a los nueve meses la expulsan de su vientre
y luego duermen venticuatro horas
como el soldado que regresa del frente.

WOMEN DON'T DIE ON THE FRONT LINES

Women don't die on the front lines,
their heads don't roll like golf balls,
they don't sleep under a forest of gunpowder,
they don't leave the sky in ruins.
No snow freezes their hearts.
Women don't die on the front lines,
they don't drive the devil out of Jerusalem,
they don't blow up aqueducts or railroads,
they don't master the arts of war
or of peace either.
They don't make generals
or unknown soldiers carved out of stone
in town squares.
Women don't die on the front lines.
They are statues of salt in the Louvre,
mothers like Phaedra,
lovers of Henry the Eighth,
Mata Haris,
Eva Peróns,
queens counselled by prime ministers,
nursemaids, cooks, washerwomen,
romantic poets.
Women don't make History,
but at nine months they push it out of their bellies
then sleep for twenty-four hours
like a soldier on leave from the front.

POETICA

La virtualidad
de un esquema hecho a pulso
permanece insensible
a una alarma de fuego.
Mi mano,
no más quieta que mis nervios,
crea el poema
moviéndose de norte a sur
como en las latitudes.

POETICS

The verisimilitude
of a sketch done right
will not give any heed
to a fire alarm.
My hand,
no calmer than my nerves,
forms the poem
moving north to south
across the latitudes.

EL TIEMPO

Asumo el tiempo
con un extraño vértigo en los ojos.
Los ancianos me dan consejos
como a un niño,
sacan a relucir viejas mentiras,
como si el polvo
no lo hubiera cubierto todo esta mañana.

TIME

I shoulder time
with vertigo in my eyes.
My elders give me advice
as if I were a child;
they brandish old lies,
as if, this morning, dust
hadn't covered everything.

COMPRO MUEBLES VIEJOS: SILLAS, CAMAS, BASTIDORES. . .

Los compradores de muebles viejos
a menudo olvidan el amor,
sustraen una cama o una silla
aprovechando que sus dueños se han mudado
para siempre,
que embarcaron con la vejez y la tarde,
que no tuvieron tiempo de decidir la suerte
de los objetos
y pa última hora hubo que deshabitar la casa,
abandonar la felicidad de antes
y partir sin despedirse de la cocinera.
Los compradores de muebles viejos
borran el polvo,
cualquier mancha de aceite sobre la superficie
y hasta inventan una historia feliz
para el nuevo dueño:
"Aquí se sentaba el Rey Midas".
"En esta cama nació María Antonieta".
Pero las huellas del antiguo cuerpo
no desaparecen nunca,
ni la fatalidad, ni la soberbia
y el nuevo propietario comienza a pensar
que él es el otro,
que todo lo que toca se convierte en sal y agua,
que su mujer ha perdido la cabeza
y que ya no hay modo de no morir como los otros.

I BUY OLD FURNITURE: CHAIRS, BEDS, BED SPRINGS...

Dealers in old furniture
are not sentimental;
they slip out with a bed or a chair
once the owners have gone away
for good,
have set forth at old age and evening,
with no time to provide
for what they own
and at the last minute have abandoned their house,
left old happiness behind,
without saying good-bye to the cook.
Dealers in old furniture
wipe off the dust
and oil spots on table tops,
make up fine stories
to tell the new owner:
"King Midas sat here."
"Marie Antoinette was born in this bed."
Still the old body's impression
never disappears,
nor its fate, nor its pride
and the new owner begins to imagine
he's the former owner,
that all he touches turns to salt and water,
that his wife has lost her head,
and he's like all the rest and can't keep from dying.

GRABADO

Landaluze el cínico pintó negras,
las hizo andar en puntillas por la casa,
les puso una flor en la boca.

Aquella tarde vio morir a Paula
encerrada en la jaula de la cotorra.
¡Somos hermosas! ¡Somos hermosas!
y el eco destrozó la vajilla de Sevres.

Aquella tarde pintó a Paula,
plumero en mano, distraída como una muerta.

ETCHING

Landaluze the cynic painted black girls;
he made them walk on tiptoe around the house;
he put a flower in each girl's mouth.

That afternoon he saw Paula die
locked up in the parrot's cage.
We're beautiful! We're beautiful!
and the echo broke the Sèvres china.

That afternoon he painted Paula,
feather duster in hand, distracted like a dead girl.

THE PATIO AT MY HOUSE

EL PATIO DE MI CASA

EN EL ARCA DE NOE

Amarrados con dura cadena
duermen el alma y su cuerpo.
El puntapié del otro
los despierta,
la mano sobre el cuello los ahoga.
"¡Tú, a la cocina —le gritan al alma—,
y tú, junto a los otros!"

Qué bien arde la gota de sangre.

IN NOAH'S ARK

Held together by a heavy chain
the soul and her body sleep.
Someone wakes them
with a kick,
a hand on their throat chokes them.
"You, to the kitchen," they shout to the soul,
"and you, get with the others!"

See how hot a drop of blood burns.

CREDO

Si es verdad que hiciste la luz
y las sombras.
Si tu voz es inaudible
y tu mirada eterna
como tú mismo,
dime, por Dios, qué hago yo aquí,
tan pequeñita,
¿aguardando el cielo o el infierno?
Por favor, olvídate de mí
para bien y para mal.
Vivir en la cabeza de un pintor, ser soñada.
Eso, sólo eso,
o una rama caída en el bosque.

CREED

If it's true you made light
and shadow.
If your voice is inaudible
and your sight eternal
like yourself,
tell me, for God's sake, what I'm doing here,
one small woman,
waiting for heaven or hell?
Please forget all about me
for better or worse.
Better to live in a painter's mind, to be dreamed.
That, only that,
or be a fallen branch in a forest.

CARTOMANCIA

En tu mano se cruzan todos los caminos.
El ferrocarril de Australia
bordea suavemente
su piel erizada de colinas.
Encima de tu mano se ha posado una cigarra
azul, que habla por boca de otro.
Si acerco el ojo la veo,
el rostro ennegrecido por el humo de la vela
que consumen la casa y el paisaje;
estás triste, lo sé,
pero, ¿quién no?
¿quién ríe y canta como si nada
en medio de los pajarracos del jardín?

FORTUNETELLING

In your hand all paths cross.
The Australian railroad
gently skirts
your skin bristling with hills.
Someone has laid a blue cigarette in your hand;
it speaks through someone else's mouth.
Leaning very close, I see that mouth,
its contours blackened by the candle's smoke
that the house and the landscape swallow up;
you're sad, I know,
but who isn't?
Who laughs and sings as if nothing were wrong
in the midst of those sly birds in the garden?

LA PATRIA DE MI MADRE

Mi madre decía siempre
que la patria era cualquier sitio,
preferiblemente el sitio de la muerte.
Por eso compró la tierra más árida
y el paisaje más triste
y la yerba más seca,
y junto al árbol infeliz
comenzó a levantar su patria.
La construía a pedazos
(un día esta pared, otro día el techo,
y a ratos, huecos para dejar colar el aire).
Mi casa es mi patria -decía-
y yo la veía cerrar los ojos
como una muchacha llena de ilusión
mientras escogía, de nuevo, a tientas,
el sitio de la muerte.

MY MOTHER'S HOMELAND

My mother always said
your homeland is any place,
preferably the place where you die.
That's why she bought the most arid land,
the saddest landscape,
the driest grass,
and beside the wretched tree
began to build her homeland.
She built it by fits and starts
  (one day this wall, another day the roof;
from time to time, holes to let air squeeze in).
My house, she would say, is my homeland,
and I would see her close her eyes
like a young girl full of dreams
while she chose, once again, groping,
the place where she would die.

GRABADO

Dos señores están sembrando
un vasto campo.
Sobre sus cabezas
pájaros negros
prueban fortuna.

ETCHING

Two men are sowing
a vast field.
Above their heads
black birds
try their luck.

LA MIRADA

Búscate, búscate en el espejo.
Esos labios crispados,
esas ojeras y esos ojos
te delatan.
Si valiera la pena
podrías desarrugar el entrecejo
y pintarte la boca de mujer.
Así sin maquillaje
intenta cruzar la calle
y siéntate junto a los arrecifes
a ver pasar los años,
su desfile de soldados
a pie, en tanques, en carretas
o en coche fúnebre.

GLANCE

Look, look at yourself in the mirror.
Those curling lips,
those dark circles, those eyes
give you away.
If you really wanted to,
you could unwrinkle your brow
and paint your mouth.
Like this, with no make-up,
go on across the street,
go sit by the reefs
and watch the years go by,
the parade of soldiers marching by,
and the tanks, and wagons,
and hearses.

FABULA

Interrogo al espejo:
—Dime, espejo mágico, ¿esa luz que se gasta
en la vela, es el alma de Fausto?
¿Y ese viento que aulla en mi puerta
nos trae malas nuevas?
¿Y ese oso de ojos torcidos
por qué tiembla y solloza?
—Señora, junto al brocal del pozo
encontrarás al cazador
convertido en ovejo.
No lo toques, no lo mires.
Debajo de su pata trae escrito un mensaje:
"mi cabeza no es mía, es del verdugo".
Aplícatelo como un bordado a tu traje de oveja.

FABLE

I ask the mirror,
"Tell me, magic mirror, that flickering candle light,
is it the soul of Faust?
Does that wind howling at my door
bring bad news?
Why does that wall-eyed bear
tremble and weep?"
"Lady, by the mouth of the well
you'll find the hunter
changed to a ram.
Don't touch him, don't look at him.
Under his hoof there's a message.
My head isn't mine, it's the hangman's.
Embroider that to your sheep's clothing."

DE LA NATURALEZA DE LA VIDA

Siempre hay un hombre pintando
la puerta de la casa,
una mujer recortando el cesped,
un viejo subiéndose al techo del garage,
un oso de hierba metiéndose en el patio,
una cabeza decapitada por la luz
estallando en llanto,
un automóvil pisoteando los instintos,
un ametrallado en la noche
y otro puesto de patas en la calle.
Siempre estás en el sueño
y estoy yo y están mis hijos
y cuando despierto
la luz es de otro mundo
y la tamiza la leve inquietud
de entrever a ratos
un paisaje verdadero.

THE NATURE OF LIFE

There's always a man painting
the door of his house,
a woman cutting the grass,
an old man climbing on to the roof of his garage,
sturdy weeds growing all over the backyard,
a head, decapitated by light,
bursting into tears,
a car flattening human instincts,
a man machine-gunned in the night
and another thrown out, on all fours, in the street.
You are always in my dream,
I am there, and my children.
When I wake up,
light is coming from another world;
a slight concern filters that light
as I catch a glimpse
of a real landscape.

NATURALEZA MUERTA

Fue el viento
quien derramó el vino sobre la mesa
(el blanco mantel ahora con huellas de sangre),
y quizás la perdiz
y el ramo de uvas verdes
   son homenajes a los misterios cotidianos,
   a la mano cercenada
   que mueve con eterno regocijo la noira,
al hombre feliz
      o acorralado
que abandona su lecho
   el mismo del amor y de la muerte,
para tocar campanas
   o amasarnos el pan de cada día,
cuando apenas se divisan tras la puerta
   perros en sombras, trasnochadores,
damiselas que escapan en pieles de serpientes,
y el astuto leproso huyendo del contagio humano.

STILL LIFE

It was the wind
that spilled the wine all over the table
(blood spots now on the white cloth).
The partridge
and the bunch of green grapes
    might be offerings to common mysteries,
    to the worn hand
    pulling the well rope, eternally rejoicing,
to the happy
        or the cornered man
who leaves the bed
    he makes love in and will die in
to ring bells
    or knead his daily bread;
through the door you can barely make out
    dogs in the shadows, sleepwalkers,
debutantes escaping in serpent skins,
the clever leper fleeing human contagion.

THANKSGIVING

Cada día la luna y el peregrino
se instalan en cualquier ciudad,
bajo una ventana y una flor,
en casas polvorientas, atestadas de voces,
de penumbras insalvables;
y cada día la muchacha tímida, de ojos cortados,
y el vagabundo sin señas, su compañero,
suben la gran escalera de caracol,
y ven desde lo más alto del pico de la montaña
un mar donde se mueren o se salvan los otros.

THANKS GIVING

Every day the moon and the pilgrim
put up in some town,
under windows with flowers,
in dusty houses filled with voices
and unconquerable shadows.
And every day the shy girl with almond eyes
and her companion, the drifter with no address,
climb the great spiral staircase.
From the highest point of the mountain, they see
an ocean where people die or save each other.

DIASPORA

No lo niego.
Somos un pueblo que huye de su destino;
cuerpos de coral
que el sueño devora
con sólo mirarlos.
No lo niego.

DIASPORA

I don't deny it.
We're a people who flee their destiny,
bodies of coral
that dreams devour
just by looking at us.
I don't deny it.

ANNE SEXTON

Mientras leía sus poemas
vi su rostro joven asomado
a la ventana,
y la hice pasar;
se sentó allí, en el sillón de mimbre,
sonriente,
casi feliz de no estar viva,
disfrutando su cigarrillo
a largas pausas,
borrando las distancias,
el puente de agua entre
ella y yo.
Eran sus ojos
depositarios entonces
de la fe, del relámpago
que da o quita la existencia.
Soñó mientras hablaba;
era la suya una voz cargada
de promesas
y la distancia infinita
la ahogaba;
se recuperó para despedirse,
volvió sus ojos a la flor
de otoño
que como ella
iba a languidecer
en un momento,
y su adiós fue casi un mensaje,
una ilusión cumplida;
pero ella está demasiado viva
para describirla en un poema.

ANNE SEXTON

While I was reading her poems,
I saw her young face
at the window;
I had her come in.
She sat there, in the wicker rocker,
smiling,
almost happy not to be alive,
enjoying her cigarette,
at long intervals,
erasing the distances,
the bridge of water between us.
Her eyes held
the faith, the lightning
that gives life or takes it.
She dreamed as she was talking;
she had a voice
charged with promises;
the infinite distance
choked her.
She recovered to say good-by,
turned her eyes to the flower
of autumn
that like her
would fade soon.
Her good-bye was almost a message,
a dream fulfilled,
but she is too alive
to describe in a poem.

MELANCOLIA I

Olvidé el poema
de la casa de La Habana
oliendo a pescado
y yo en el rincón del baño
lavando y llorando en silencio
mientras la radio proclama
un mundo que ya no existe.

MELANCHOLY I

I've forgotten the poem
about the house in Havana
smelling of fish
and me in a corner of the bathroom
washing and crying in silence
while the radio proclaims a world
that doesn't exist any more.

ORDEN DEL DIA

Ella necesita un sombrero
tan elegante
como para presentarse
ante el Presidente
de no sé qué institución benéfica,
pero en realidad, se trata de una orden,
algo que ella no asimila del todo
porque está dicho con una sonrisa.
Así nos pasa a todos.

ORDER OF THE DAY

She needs a hat
elegant enough
to make her presentable
to the President
of who knows what charitable organization.
Truth is, it's more an order than invitation,
something she doesn't quite pick up on,
because they say it with a smile.
It happens like that to all of us.

ANUNCIO PAGADO

Se suplica a los duendes de piel aterciopelada,
a los muchachones sedientos de historia,
a los jueces también de lo Divino,
que dejen hablar
a las viejas señoras de sayas plisadas,
a los débiles,
a los de uñas carcomidas,
a los niños vapuleados
y crecidos en cárceles maternas.
Será un modo de sacarlos a todos
de sus cuevas.

PAID ANNOUNCEMENT

We ask the phantoms with velvety skin,
the young kids trying to make names for themselves,
even judges in High Places,
to give equal time
to old ladies in pleated skirts,
the weak,
people with chewed-up nails,
children abused
and raised in maternal prisons.
Maybe that way we can bring them
out of their caves.

BIOGRAPHICAL NOTE

Belkis Cuza Malé was born on June 15, 1942 in Guantánamo, Cuba, the daughter of a cement-factory worker. Encouraging the zeal she'd had for writing since her childhood, her family sent her to private schools, particularly those catering to children of professionals and bureaucrats, and finally for a master's degree in Hispanic American and Cuban literature from the Universidad del Oriente, in 1964.

Following graduation, Cuza Malé moved to Havana where she wrote for two years as a radio and television critic for the Communist newspaper *Hoy*. From 1966 to 1968, she worked as editor of the cultural pages of *Granma*, the offical organ of the Communist party of Cuba. During that time, two of her collections of poems, *Tiempo del sol* and *Cartas a Ana Frank*, were awarded mentions by Casa de las Americas in 1963. Also, in 1966, Cuza Malé married poet Heberto Padilla. She continued to write and edit for the literary journal, *La Gaceta de Cuba*, published by the Union of Writers and Artists of Cuba.

With the change in the mood of Cuba in the 60s and 70s, the fortunes of Cuza Malé and Padilla also changed. In 1971 both were jailed for what the government called subversive writing. While they were soon released, their lives were overshadowed by censorship and house arrest. Cuza Malé's manuscript, *Juego de damas*, a finalist for another Casa de las Americas award in 1968, was in press at the time of the couple's arrest and was shredded by censors almost as soon as it came out. To date, Cuza Malé's mature writing has only been published in anthologies and literary journals in both Spanish and English. This collection, published with the assistance of the Witter Bynner Foundation for Poetry, includes the suppressed *Juego de damas* Cuban work as well as poems written since her arrival in the United States in 1979.

Belkis Cuza Malé now lives with her husband and her son in Princeton, New Jersey. She continues to write poetry, and she has also completed two novels and a biography of Juana Borrero. Additionally she edits a bilingual literary magazine, *Linden Lane Magazine*, a review of Latin American and North American writers.